Unconditional 2, Four by Four - The Baby Daddy Drama Trauma!

TAWANA ROQUALL FULTZ

Copyright © July 2021 by Tawana Roquall Fultz

Copyright © July 2021 by Tawana Roquall Fultz
Publisher: B'ABLE PRODUCTS, LLC

All rights reserved. No part of this publication may be reproduced, distributed, or transmitted in any form or by any means, including photocopying, recording, or other electronic or mechanical methods, without the prior written permission of the publisher, except in the case of brief quotations embodied in critical reviews and certain other noncommercial uses permitted by copyright law.

Published in the United States of America
First Edition, 2021
Paperback ISBN: 978-7368398-0-2
Library of Congress Control Number: 2021914698

Cover by: Ruth Adedeji
Editor: Genevieve A. Scholl
Formatted by: Genevieve A. Scholl

TABLE OF CONTENTS

ACKNOWLEDGEMENTS 5
INTRODUCTION 6
BABY DADDY 8
Chapter One: Unconditional Freedom 9
Chapter Two: Redemption of My Sins 18
DRAMA 26
Chapter Three: Peace Offering 28
TRAUMA 48
Chapter Four: The Drama Trauma 50
ABOUT THE AUTHOR 81

ACKNOWLEDGEMENTS

First and foremost, I would like to give honor to God for being everything I need and for being merciful towards me in my most uncompromising and darkest hours. This book is dedicated to all the single mothers out there with multiple children by multiple men and still have dreams and pursuing them. Also giving honor to those single mothers and fathers who choose to stick around and tough it out for the sake of the family structure as well. More importantly, to my children and every other young adult in need of understanding and clarity on what not to do as a man, father, woman or mother. Moreover, I would like to say that truth is necessary and forgiveness is possible when you begin to see things the way they were intended. Lastly, but not least. I would like to acknowledge every eye and every heart that has opened up to hear my story. I pray that you will all be given wisdom, knowledge and understanding in all things and be blessed. Amen.

INTRODUCTION

It was truly the unconditional love of God moving in some unconditional circumstances that brought me and my children through. I would like to share with you how I became the mother of four children by four different baby daddies and all drama and trauma that came with it. Many times, one's path, trials, and tribulations ultimately prepare us in order to propel us into destiny and purpose. In a society that has already counted her out as a contributor to the economic growth and success, I am determined to prove that even though we make poor decisions and even delays and detours along the way, God does have a way of working it all out eventually. I need for someone experiencing physical and mental abuse to know that you are not alone. It was scary, it was hard, but I would not trade my children in for anything in the world, and I have learned to forgive my abusers. but, most importantly, I forgave myself.

This is a cry out, for a second chance. For every girl, boy, man, and woman that did not give up or throw in the towel but made it to the other side of the trauma and are ready to begin a new life with wisdom, knowledge, and understanding. I also want to acknowledge the fact that every woman who is experiencing this kind of trauma is not just statistically projected products of our environments, but we are also strong women who desire the best life has to offer. Although, some choices in life can stagnant a person, tenacity and determination can help you overcome these obstacles and bring yourself back into alignment with the divine plan and purpose for your life. It's a warning to be patient, do your research and background checks on a potential spouse, stay connected to the ones who love you most, and never settle for less than the Lord has already promised you!

This book details the innocence, betrayals, and growing pains at a more personal level. I promised that I would go further into details about the men, the abuse, the drama, and the trauma and how it affected me, my children, and my life as a whole. Prepare yourself to go back there with me, and let's learn how to forgive ourselves together.

BABY DADDY

Chapter One

UNCONDITIONAL FREEDOM

From as far back as I can remember, I've always said that I was never going to have kids. Every so often my mom still reminds me of how I said this growing up and ended up with four kids by four baby daddies. Although my children were not planned pregnancies, I do believe that each one of them are predestined and called according to a purpose. I do remember thinking to myself as a young girl that if I ever had children, I'd make sure that they'd love me unconditionally, as I do them, and we would be a team. Or should I say a force to be reckoned with. But the idea of having someone love me unconditionally wasn't the only reason I entertained the thoughts of children.

I also knew that having a child could speed up the process of getting into my own place. I will admit that I really just wanted to be grown and free to do whatever I wanted. But of course I learned very quickly that there is no freedom in the rearing of children. Although my children are all grown up now and are in college, they have been a complete blessing to me and I would not exchange them for anything

Unconditional 2, Four by Four – The Baby Daddy Drama Trauma

in the world. My children not only give my life meaning but they also have been one of the guiding forces that helped me to make wiser decisions along the way.

As I told you in the first edition, I found out I was pregnant with my first child after my eighteenth birthday party. After having up to one hundred guys show up to my birthday party and dancing and the roof off the building, I finally moved from that apartment I had shared with baby daddy Number One. I met 'Number One' one day while walking home from school. I was in high school at the time, about sixteen years old, and he was maybe nineteen or twenty. My sister thought he was so cute because it was every girl's dream during those days to have a light-skinned, hazel-eyed boyfriend. Although I was a bit young to be dating him, I would sneak over his house and hide in his bedroom down in the basement to visit him.

The basement of his house was where everyone entertained their guests, and his mom would only come down to wash a load of clothes. We also had some mutual friends, a couple that lived down the street from my house. We would chill there sometimes often just drinking beer, smoking weed, and cigarettes. Remember the couple's house where my mom came beating on the door looking for me and I hid from her inside, telling everyone to keep quiet? Everyone was so afraid that my mom would come back with the police.

Soon, another couple moved in a few houses down from them and we became friends with them as well. Because I was only sixteen,

I had to be in the house early and, eventually, Number One had taken a liking to the woman that had just moved in down the street. I noticed, became jealous, and then decided to flirt with our mutual friend, Chris, to get even. We were all at the Cody High School football field, drinking beer and hanging out. I decided I wanted to make Number One jealous, just to take his attention away from the new girl. So, I walked over to Chris and started dancing on him and being really flirtatious. I made sure Number One was looking at me and then I gave Chris a big sloppy kiss!

Chris was a handsome, tall, slim, white boy. He kind of resembled one of my favorites actors that played the character Rocky Balboa, and he was very cute. Number One got so mad that he walked over to me and grabbed me by my hair and slammed my face into the bleacher seat pole and would not have stopped if they didn't get me lose from him. My forehead grew so fast I looked like the elephant woman. There's still a small knot on my forehead to this day.

After about a week, the blood then drained into both my eyes and I had nose bleeds every other day until my forehead healed. It was one of the most painful and embarrassing incidents that happened in my life.

I was not allowed outside after that for a while. I would just sit in the living room window watching them all walk back and forth to the store for beer. After about a week, Number One had moved in with the new girl on the block and I then began seeing them walking to the

Unconditional 2, Four by Four – The Baby Daddy Drama Trauma

store as well. I can remember thinking: *Lord, how is he able to walk off in the sunset with another girl after what he did to me?*

I ended up leaving town not too long after that, to finish my G.E.D at the Indiana Atterbury Job Corps. It didn't take long before I was suspended from there and sent right back home within ninety days. Back hanging out with the couple that lived a few houses down the street and Number One again.

During that time, I got a call from an ex, saying he was in town with no vehicle, but wanted to hookup. In search for a ride, we ended up on a double date with Number One and a friend of his, a girl I had never met before.

We sat at the table in my sister's apartment to play a card game of spades. Waited until everyone was buzzing good from the weed and alcohol and then snuck off into the bathroom and had some hot, passionate sex. We put hickies all over each other's neck, and then returned back to the table as if nothing ever happened. It was how we rolled considering he was only in town for a short time. Number One was so drunk, he never noticed a thing.

Nevertheless, a few months later, I ended up getting hired at a nursing home with Number One's mother. It was a midnight shift and because I was only sixteen, I had to be emancipated to work there. Emancipated meant to be considered an adult before the age of eighteen, my mom agreed to sign over all her parental legal rights. Once I became a legal adult at sixteen, almost seventeen, I began to look for my first apartment. I was now working with Number One's mother, aunts, and even a few cousins, and, maybe eight months later, Number One and I decided to get an apartment together.

It was our very first apartment. I was so excited; I just wanted to be grown! Number One and I were at the rental office completing some paperwork and getting the keys. During this process, Number One started to gaze off with a blank stare and just shut down. I had to finish the paperwork for him, but later asked him what had happened. He explained he had some type of anxiety when in the spot light or too much attention from people.

The drama began the night we invited his brother and his brother's girlfriend over to see our new apartment. Somehow, his brother and I got into a disagreement and I told him to leave. As I was escorting him out the door, he swung and hit me in the chin. I was livid! How dare a man hit me, in front of my so-called boyfriend and in our own home? Mind you, it was Number One's older brother, and I looked at him, expecting him to do something! The moment I saw that Number One was afraid of his brother and did nothing, I knew I was through!

We put in our thirty-day notice; Number One moved out first and I moved out a couple weeks later after my eighteenth birthday party that I had already planned previously. It was a party to remember, as I told you in my first edition of Unconditional. I had previously put in for another apartment and was on the waiting list, so I decided to check the status of that application. I was told I could move in within the next thirty days, and stayed at my mom's until then. It was at my mom's that I started to get sick and decided to go to the doctor.

I was told I was two to three weeks pregnant, and after I told Number One, I instantly knew I no longer wanted to be with him, and I never touched him again. It's something about that first response from a man, when you first tell him that you are pregnant. If it's anything other than love, excitement, and affection, you become completely turned off to the point of no return. However, I did enjoy a surprise baby shower that was given by my cousin, Trecey, at the end of my pregnancy. Although no one showed up but my aunt, I am ever so grateful to my cousin for the thoughtfulness, time, and effort she put into that special time for me.

Two weeks after my baby was born, Number One asked to come by to visit. It had to be about midnight by the time he arrived, but once he was there, he asked if he could take his son to see his mom. It was late but I allowed him to take the baby, after he'd begged and promised me he would keep him safe. It had to have been only an hour or so since he had left before he was calling back and saying he was on his way back. I couldn't believe he was still out driving with my newborn baby. I was livid but grateful to have my baby back home safe with me.

I can remember thinking, *Did she put my newborn baby out of her house? Why not wait until later that morning to bring him home?* It was never explained, but I just knew that my baby was not accepted and the family had doubts whether it was actually Number One's biological child. After three attempts to prove paternity, and three no-shows, a support order was granted by default.

My son did eventually get a chance to get to know his dad a little later on as he grew older. He'd asked if he could take our son to Florida for a summer visit, which was extended, but shortly ended unexpectedly after his dad became divorced and homeless. My son shares often of some good memories he has with his dad, and it makes me happy to know it wasn't all bad for him as a child. However, as I grow and observe over the years, I am amazed at all of the many ways our choices can affect our children rather positively or negatively.

It wasn't until our son's high school graduation that I really reached out to Number One or his family. I drove to their homes and personally invited them all, gave them all free tickets, but no one showed up. I feel it was truly their loss, but since then, they have managed to build a decent relationship over the years and I won't complain. I just figured the Lord allowed me to have the best years of his life all to myself, and I appreciate every minute of it. My firstborn, my first love, and he has been a complete blessing to me. Never given me any trouble growing up.

Number One paid his child support the majority of the time, and I was fine with that. It just made me sad sometimes when he'd see his

Unconditional 2, Four by Four – The Baby Daddy Drama Trauma

brothers coming and going with their dads and he'd be left behind with me. But I always made sure he had just the same as the other brothers and they would share with him as well. There was never much between Number One as far as a relationship. He was a quiet guy with a big temper, daydreamed a lot, but never really was my type at all.

However, I'm sure now that it would take a strong, loud, confident praying man to be able to keep my attention. I was never in love with Number One. I believe I had a crush that was short lived and forgotten the moment I found out I was pregnant. After the physical abuse, and basically denying my baby in the beginning, it makes it a bit uncomfortable to engage on any level. You eventually learn to forgive but never forget.

Being a mom for the first time was hard for me in the beginning, just trying to adjust to the changes that I had no idea I had to make. Things like going to the bathroom while holding a newborn was not expected in the least. Moreover, I never anticipated all the things I would have to pack every time I wanted to leave and go somewhere. The pain was real, and I could not anticipate the recovery stages and how I would able to get through it. It was very hard for me to understand how they just send you home from the hospital right after you're done giving birth … alone.

I was so weak and tired, I thought I would have time to regain my strength and health before I would be left home alone with such a tiny baby, I knew nothing about. I guess now, hind sight, it was beautiful how we began to know each other. Identifying the wines from the grunts and groans was actually amazing and although it takes time to learn our babies, I always consider my firstborn my first love. He's all grownup now, a very unique young man, and building his own empire right now. It was only by the grace of God that I was able to keep my child and see him become a man and I give all the glory to him alone.

Chapter Two

REDEMPTION OF MY SINS

My first child was about seven years old when I moved to Southwest Detroit. I had a medical assistant job working at a family practice nearby, and that's where I met Number Two. He came into the office one day, and the next, he was calling in asking to speak to me, saying he was my secret admirer. Number Two was tall, light-skinned known drug dealer in the neighborhood with twelve kids by ten different women. He played the secret admirer game for about four to six weeks, before finally admitting who he really was.

Although he was a so-called thug, I thought I was just as tough and ready for whatever came my way. Needless to say, I figured out that after about a month or so of talking to him on the phone, sending flowers and lunch to my job, I eventually wanted to meet him in person despite his background. He was a very sharp dresser and loved to show off his money and spoil his women. For some reason, I always loved a challenge and enjoyed having the man that all the women wanted. The competition was real, and it made me feel superior to watch other women plot, plan, and lust over the man that wanted me.

Although I was with a very well-known brother and I was the chosen queen of the day, it wasn't long before I started to see why it may not have been wise to date a drug dealer. He was also known for running from the police and getting away, rather in a vehicle or on foot. At the time, I was not looking for love, nor was I trying to start any kind of relationship with anyone. But rather just trying to have a one-night-stand with this street thug, just to knock the edge off. My rule was, "Do not fall in love!", because I was emotionally unavailable and desperately in need of some real soul searching and healing in my life.

It was risky, but he had a little money, loved to spoil his women, and, plus, I always did like playing close to the edge. After a few months of the free weed, surprise lunches, multiple rides here and there, I began to get a bit lonely … and horny. Completely entertaining the lustful thoughts of getting a quicky, but not realizing how terribly dangerous that could be. Meaning, it comes with a whole lot more than you're ever willing to consider or sacrifice, and then, he played the oldest trick in the book on me.

He waited until I was enjoying myself and stopped in the middle of sex and said, "I can't feel nothing."

He then asked if he could take the condom off. I was pissed, because it had been a while since I had been touched by a man, and my body wanted some relief. The moment I said, "Okay, but please be careful," I knew then, the Lord had just turned the fire up in my life and would begin to purify my soul. Soon, I would be screaming, "Merciful Lord, forgive me!"

John 15: 1-8 KJV. "I am the true vine, and my Father is the husbandman. ²Every branch in me that beareth not fruit he taketh away: and every branch that beareth fruit, he purgeth it, that it may bring forth more fruit."

Hallelujah!

It didn't take long before I was taking a pregnancy test at work and discovering my fate. I planned to have yet another abortion, but this time, I had a really bad dream the night before the scheduled procedure. It literally felt like the Lord had visited me just to remind me that I had had six abortions previously and that this one would be number seven. There I was, pregnant by this one-night-stand, and it was truly a nightmare from Elm's Street. I was completely embarrassed to be pregnant by him, and the fear of the Lord's wrath was weighing heavy in my heart and in my mind.

Conflicted inside, I didn't want to abort yet another innocent child due to my own negligence. Because of the dream I had from God, and something about the number seven, made it just that much easier to keep the baby and do the right thing. I knew one thing for sure, and that was, I could never kill an innocent baby just to keep a man or please a man. The dream had also showed me how very special and gifted the child would be to my life and how important it was to keep him no matter who or what I had to lose in the process. I had a home and a job, and there were no excuses to abort this time as I had before.

After a terrifying night of fighting with Number Two, there was a horrific freak accident up the street from my block. It was with the woman who I caught him with in my kitchen a few months earlier. It was during the drag races on Fort Street one night. It was the most unbelievable scene you could ever imagine. The cars took off, and one of the drivers lost control of his vehicle and hit this young lady at full speed.

Her body was severed in two, and her torso was thrown across the street into another parking lot. The lower part of her body was still standing there for a few moments and then fell to the ground. It was the most gruesome sight, and everyone was taking pictures in disbelief.

Drag racing is common in most neighborhoods in the City of Detroit, and it happens very late at night. If you listen closely, you can hear the tires burning rubber on the concrete in the late-night early morning hours no matter what area you live in.

This horrific night will never be forgotten, and I pray that everyone affected by that tragic night be healed and given wisdom when participating in these activities. I eventually moved in with a friend after my baby's delivery. But later found myself moving back in with my ex due to me not wanting to be a burden on someone with children. Number Two paid child support and was able to send clothes and diapers in bulk from time to time, which helped me out a lot in the long run. As my son grew older, he did begin to build a relationship with his dad and with his now fourteen sisters and brothers from his dad's side of the family.

My son is indeed special and anointed and always behaved well beyond his years. He graduated from Cass Tech High with honors, college credits, and a full-ride football scholarship.

Unfortunately, his dad belled out on him shortly before his high school graduation and things just continued to get worst between them. During our son's college football seasons, his dad tried to jump back into his life as his football manager. However, after a re-structured ankle surgery, our son decided to stop playing for a while.

Because of the abuse I suffered from Number Two, I have never really communicated with him again either. Once the boys were able to talk to their fathers, I no longer engaged on any level.

I give God all the glory for allowing me to keep my relationship with their fathers separate, and always encouraged and supported their time spent together. Although the pain and disrespect continued, I mad sure the boys called and acknowledged their dads on all holidays, birthdays, and special occasions. Nevertheless, I didn't get that same respect in return. But I do know where my help comes from, and I will continue to look to the hills. **Psalm 121:1-8 KJV**

Moreover, Number Two had so many kids, there was no way he could give our child the time and attention he really needed, and I am so sorry for that.

I would like to share the fact that we as women really need to think more outside the box when it comes to bringing a child into the world under these dysfunctional circumstances. There is so much more to consider when deciding to rear up a child, other than cost and matrimony. It never dawned on me that the child may have some kind of resentment for being a child of circumstance and not of a union. Having feelings of depression, anger, and feeling unloved or unwanted by the estranged parent is very real. Or even feelings of not being valued or having any importance and priority that comes with being a child.

For example, you may begin to hear questions about why the estranged parent is unable to reciprocate the love and engage with the child. Questions like: 'is he really my dad' and 'why did you choose him to have a child with?' Again, experiencing the differences and comparing their relationship to the other children and their dads. It is very hard and sad to watch your son or daughter want and need their dad or mom and maybe blame you for the disconnection. It is also very possible for the child to think of their own life as a mistake that should not have happened, which may, in turn, prevent them from thriving in life and, instead, be crippled by the circumstances at hand.

My thoughts never even reached that magnitude when I decided to bring children into this cold-cold world. My fear was more focused on the mean and cruel ways of ending a pregnancy, rather than the future outcomes of it all. So, this is yet another cry out to my sisters

Unconditional 2, Four by Four – The Baby Daddy Drama Trauma

and brothers, bringing awareness to other extenuating factors that would cause you to think a little more carefully about having unprotected sex. I just feel like if things were explained to me to this magnitude, I would have been more prepared for motherhood. I am absolutely sure that my children were and still are being affected negatively by some of my past choices and decisions in men.

Another extenuating facture is the rearing, the values and spiritual beliefs that tend to collide at any given moment. For instance, one of my sons asked me why I tell him to pray, no fighting, and notify an adult, but when he goes to his dad's, he's punished for not fighting back. I have had one of my sons ask me, 'Why are the rules so much different at dad's house and so strict when at mom's?' It eventually forced my children to re-evaluate who was the good or bad parent and also decided what level of respect would be given to the more passive or disconnected parent. Once a child decides that you are not accountable or dependable, a surge of disrespect and the challenging of your intelligence and authority is on the rise.

Moreover, I want to help you think twice about who you're having these children with. One of the most irritating things about having multiple baby daddies is having to deal with every other woman that comes into their lives. After the first ten women, the pattern became more and more clear to me that I would relive this nightmare over and over till the children became adults. Seemed like every woman after me needed to know why we broke up and needed to make sure that I didn't want them back. Not only that, I spent a lot of time in the courthouse fighting for sole-custody, child support, and scheduled visitation orders.

Being a baby mama was one of the greatest challenges I ever had to master quickly or be swallowed up by the insecurities of every woman after me. It was unbelievable how the women would plot and scheme against me to ensure that their relationship wasn't being threatened. They would stick their tongues down my baby daddies' throats whenever I came near, finding all kinds of ways to keep me at bay and far away from my children and their fathers. I never understood why they felt the need to do these things, because I never gave them one inclination that I would ever touch, let alone take these men back into my life again.

It also amazes me how the other woman, or the next woman, never acknowledges the reasons why it didn't work out with the previous relationship. Was it easier to believe the I just left a good man and wonderful father for my children? I mean, like, who leaves a good man? Ladies, we must consider the previous relationship. Yes, women tend to add things in hopes of you losing interest, but please learn how to read between the lines. Every woman wants a good man and a father in the home with her children.

I am not a single parent because I want to be, and I have tried multiple things to keep the kids' father in the home. The majority of the time, the baby mama is the one who ends the relationship in the first place, at least in all of my cases anyway. Ladies, most of us left for reasons that were complete deal breakers and were forced to put the best interest of the children ahead of our own desires. But for the life of me, I will never understand why a woman would want to compete with the biological mom for the child's affection. It's a battle that cannot be won, and any man that would allow his new woman to challenge or disrespect the mother's authority is not a man or a father and vice-versa!

Nothing in the world can make a child love you more than their own mom, especially a praying mom such as myself. You will begin to understand what I mean by this in the next chapter as I explain the drama and trauma of it all.

DRAMA

Chapter Three

PEACE OFFERING

Number Three and I met on the westside of Detroit as I was walking down Grand River Ave to the corner store. He did a U-turn in the middle of the street, parked, got out of his car, and proceeded to go into the store with us. Number Three was tall, dark, and handsome with a very charming personality. But I told him that I was in an entanglement with someone else, and I wasn't ready to leave him. Number Three would not take no for answer and decided to make me this proposition that ended up costing me more than I was ever willing to give up.

He stated that if he could only have me for two weeks, he'd take that! Offering me his own vehicle to drive and taking care of all of my expenses I incurred along the way. It seemed too good to be true, but I figured since he was a few years my senior, he could handle this type of a relationship. No strings attached; friends with benefits. That's all. It wasn't long before he had taken me to his bank teller and told them that I would be depositing all of his paychecks and added me to his account.

Tawana Roquall Fultz

This was my first time ever having a real gentleman—very charming and extremely generous with his money. I hadn't been spoiled by a man like this before, so I had to rethink our entanglement arrangement a few times. Although he seemed to be every woman's dream, I was very skeptical of someone willing to pay for love and affection from a complete stranger. It didn't stop me from taking his money, but I could only imagine how easy it would be for him to cheat or fall in love with another woman. Even though he was a nice handsome man, I was not in love with him, and it was just not in the cards for us.

I think Number Three knew there was nothing he could do to win my heart because money can't buy true love. Number Three was a workaholic, but he had a beautiful little girl that he did try to make time for. He was also a quiet, introverted person who loved to eat and read books in his free time. I will admit that Number Three was very close to what I wanted my dream man to look like, but emotionally, there were no strong connections. Tall, jet-black skin, baby faced, built like machinery, yet missing a few, but one of the most important factors of all: a spiritual foundation!

To make sure Number Three did not get too attached to me, I would do little things to keep him at bay. For instance, for one of his birthdays, I paid strippers to entertain him and all his co-workers. It was a wild but great night and the girls were some of which I worked with from time to time. The girls were paid for three to four hours, anything goes, and I stayed in the back bedroom the entire time, sipping and smoking.

I told him to enjoy himself with his friends, and I did not come out until the girls were ready to leave. Oh, my mistake. I did come out one time to pee, and I saw a young lady standing on the dining room table, butt naked with one leg in the air!

One of his friends yelled out to me, "Thank you! This is the best party ever!" I know his friends thought he had the coolest girlfriend ever.

Although he spoiled me rotten, paid me weekly, and was very nice looking and charming, he still knew how to bury a bone in the yard. Actually, I caught him quite a few times in full creep mode. This one time I will never forget. It was at one of my first son's birthday parties. There I was, trying to use his camcorder to record the cartoon characters dancing with my son.

I was trying to view the footage and obviously rewound the tape back too far. The moment I pressed play, there he was, screwing this chick in the anus point blank! I could not believe my eyes. I watched for a minute until he noticed that I was too quiet and seemed to be taking longer than expected. I guess he thought about it and immediately snatched the camera from me.

I then gave him 'the look' and walked back outside with the guests and tried to keep my composure at least until the next day. In that moment, I was just reassured that he was not the one for me.

However, while he was still in creep mode and we were living together in the Detroit Bright moor Community, one time, he decided he couldn't take it anymore. Number Three gave me half of the rent money and told me to get the rest the best way I could, then left. It's funny how the strangest opportunities of situations would present themselves at the most convenient times.

After he left, I decided to call the weed man to bring me a bag so that I could sit and figure out what I wanted to do. I did not know if I wanted to pay the rent or just use the money to move away all together. When the weed man came, we begin talking and I was telling him how I was left. We laughed, but then he suggested yet another proposition. He stated that he would be glad to help and give me the other half, a favor for a favor.

You know what that meant, and, yep, I made that money. But the most fascinating part of this story is that the weed man was at least three-hundred and fifty pounds. I had no idea how we were going to pull it off, but the doggy style position seemed best for my survival from being crushed or suffocated. This was the largest man I had ever been with in my life, and I was sure that I would not feel a thing and it would be extremely quick. Lo and behold, the man was absolutely amazing!

He rearranged my furniture, blew my mind, and had me grabbing for things that were not there! So, ladies, please do not let them fat rolls fool you! That man handled his business, and I have a new respect for the full and obese man.

Well, I paid the rent and Number Three eventually came back puzzled at how all was well—rent paid, house clean, and groceries in the fridge. I really do apologize for my savage behavior and have truly repented for the willingness to accept such a proposition. Ladies, we need to understand that there is no price for your soul.

You are priceless, and to even put a number on your virtue is true blindness to self-worth, God, His word, and the multitude of spirits you tie to your soul.

Speaking of spirits, it wasn't long before another episode with Number Three. I don't know what spirit jumped out of me, but I was arriving at Number Three's house, which he shared with a male roommate at the time. As I pulled up to park in front of the house, there was another car parking as well. I didn't think anything of it at first until we both began walking up the same driveway to the side door.

Then I thought maybe she's here for his roommate, but as I approached the door, getting closer to her, I recognized who she was. Badda Boom, Badda Bing! It was a woman I had caught him with previously, and I actually chased them in his car together. I couldn't catch them that day but I got a good look at her face. Once it dawned on me, my reflexes just popped off! Somehow, my hand instantly bawled and socked her in the face. This woman was at least six feet and about two-twenty.

It was about three weeks after I gave birth to our son, and I guess I was in postpartum mode and having flashbacks. All I could hear was my oldest son hanging out the car window yelling, "Mama stop, mama stop!" I eventually had her pinned on the ground. Imagine this: me on top with my knee on her chest, she had my hair with one hand, and I had her other hand pinned with my teeth embedded in her fingers, threatening to chew them off if she didn't let my hair go! Number Three heard the commotion and came outside to see what the noise was about. He thought I had met my match and was the one on the ground.

You should've seen his face while he was begging me to get up off her. I am by no means proud of that moment and I do realize that I was completely out of control. After that, I found out that he was planning to marry this woman, so I made plans to destroy the wedding before it even happened. The anger was real because the moment I told him that I was pregnant, just like the others, he had asked me to get an abortion. His sister actually called me and told me that I was not going to trap her brother with a baby and an abortion would be wise as well.

Moreover, they were not accepting of his daughter at all or my son at first, and even told me not to name my son after him because he hated his name. Regrettably, we ended up back together again but not before the next episode that would take the drama to the next level.

Later on that year, I had an audition in Chicago at the Navy Pier, and all went up in smoke that weekend. From the moment the Greyhound bus departed, Number Three was planning his revenge.

Unconditional 2, Four by Four – The Baby Daddy Drama Trauma

I was so excited about the audition, I literally turned my cell off the moment I arrived at the downtown Chicago W. Hotel. The first night in Chicago was very long due to the long lines for the audition's registration process. When I finally returned back to my room and turned my cell phone back on, there were several voicemails from Number Three, and as I listened to them, he was singing, "Fire, Fire." I didn't think too much about it because I was really enjoying myself and it was truly a chance of a lifetime. After that long and exciting weekend, I couldn't wait to get back and start working on my new album.

When I arrived home, everything looked fine because the house was made of brick, which does not burn. I put my key in the door, opened it, and everything was pitch black. Number Three had set all my things on fire. He took my clothes, broke off the heels of my shoes, and place them all in a pile, along with my wedding dress, and set them on fire in the living room. He then took a pringles can, stuffed it with newspapers, and attempted to make a bomb by placing it by the furnace and turning the gas on, I later learned.

I could not believe my eyes, and because the house was brick and tightly closed up, the fire had smothered itself and was unable to spread to the attached duplex on the other side. The man had truly lost his mind, and I was on a mission to help him find it, in prison for sure. However, I was livid. Everything inside my home was destroyed along with all my kids' stuff as well. Immediately, I called anyone who would listen! From the fire department arson unit, down to his mother whom lived out of state. By the time I was done making calls, there were warrants for his arrest, his driver's license was locked, and he was calling leaving crying messages this time, begging me to get the police off his tail.

It wasn't long before I forgave him, but it was definitely after he replaced everything I lost in the fire. Without my testimony, they were unable to prosecute him, which eventually prevented him from going to jail for a very long time. The gratitude was short lived, but I had no home anymore, which forced me to go back to live with him yet again. I began plotting against him after those shenanigans.

One day, I was getting ready for church, and I asked Number Three if he wanted to go with me, but he insisted that he was tired and just wanted to stay in bed until I returned.

Somehow, I forgot my bible or something and had to circle back to the house. As I was about to turn onto the side street of our block, I saw Number Three at the bus stop! Dressed and on the move to visit his anal friend from the video, a.k.a. his daughter's godmother. She would bring him lunch to his job everyday as if I didn't even exist.

One day, I confronted her, and she told me flat out that they had been together for over fifteen years. He worked two jobs, they just bought a house together, and the car he was driving was in her name.

She invited me to her house to show me the paperwork, and after I saw them, I invited her to our home together. I planned for her to arrive at our house a half hour before he came home from work. After we shared information and put the lies together that he was telling both of us, we waited for him to come home. He finally arrived and walked in the door.

Once he saw her in our house, he immediately asked me, "What is she doing here?" and told her to leave.

Then I said, "No. We need to discuss what she told me."

He immediately walked out the door, trying to escape.

She walked out, left, and Number Three and I were at it again. Only a few weeks later, I caught his car at her house. This time, I just picked up the biggest brick I could find and tossed it right through her living room picture window, shattering it completely. He beat me back to the house and never spoke a word. He was giving me the silent treatment because he had to repair that window. I just wanted him to know that I knew, so that it would be that much easier to leave and move on with my life.

Over the seven years I had stayed with Number Three, off and on, I learned that money, fancy restaurants, trips around the world, and financial stability did not and would not bring happiness into my life.

Moreover, I had everything I wanted materialistically and financially, but the heart can only truly love one, and it belonged to another. There was absolutely nothing he could do to win me over, unfortunately, and it wasn't long before I started to get a little paranoid. One day, I was talking about how we needed to thank the Lord for waking us up every morning and that we would be nothing without the Lord.

Immediately, Number Three stopped me and said, "I set my alarm clock every morning, and that's how I get up every day."

I looked at him in disbelief, and asked him, "What did you just say?"

As he repeated himself, I was thinking, *Wow. I have never heard anyone speak in such disregard of the father in heaven, the creator*, and I was completely puzzled and pissed. I became more and more depressed, but I knew for sure that he was not the man for me and no amount of money in the world could make me happy with him. I would lock myself in the bathroom, turn on the sink and the shower water, so that no one could hear me, and cry my eyes out.

Sometimes, I would play loud music in the basement and sing at the top of my lungs, praying God would hear me. I was truly miserable while trying to be with a man only for his money. He was charming at times, but really, he was just another trickster that stayed way too long. I hated what I was doing, and I was constantly looking for ways to get out on my own and get rid of him once and for all.

When I finally found an apartment, I thought I would pay the rent, furnish it the way I like, before I let him know about it and move-in. After finding my apartment and paying the rent for a few months in advance, Number Three found out my secret when the rental receipt was mailed to our house. That expeditated my move.

Unconditional 2, Four by Four – The Baby Daddy Drama Trauma

After moving in my apartment, I ran into an old friend who always wanted to manage my singer career. Although I wanted to record some of the songs I had written, it was a bit challenging driving back and forth from his studio in Pontiac, MI to my new apartment in Inkster, MI. Eventually, we decided that it would be better if I moved to Pontiac, closer to the studio. Because my children were with their dads for the summer, I moved again quickly before the next school year would start and the boys would return home.

During that time, I discovered I was pregnant with Number Three's baby. It was not planned either, but this son was extremely special.

My third son was born exactly four days after my birthday, and I thought that was special in itself. I couldn't wait to see who he would act like and resemble the most. It seemed like I would have so much in common with him, by sharing such close birthdays together. When he was born, he had to be observed closely due to him swallowing some of the placenta fluids during birth. And because I had other school aged children at home unattended during my delivery, Number Three and I had to take turns visiting our baby in the hospital after my discharge.

Thankfully, his hospital stay was only a few days longer than mine, and my delivery was quick and much easier the third time around. One of the days I was at the hospital to visit our son, the nurse accidentally got me mixed up with the other woman Number Three had at the hospital with him earlier that day. It still amazes me how, where, and when men decide to cheat and humiliate you. He turned out to be a halfway decent father, but please believe me when I say it took all of Jesus and his disciples to keep the casualties at a minimum. What I've learned is, everyone has their own way of parenting and we need to know these things about a person before sex.

It was our son's first grade year and I had enrolled him in the school directly across the street from my new apartment. It would have been the first time that he would be in the same school as one of his older brothers. We both agreed that I would not file for child support and when they set the court date, I would let them know that Number Three bought everything our son needed and there was no need for an order at that time. Obviously, he was very paranoid and thought I would have him paying one hundred and seventy-five dollars every week like he was paying for his daughter the entire eighteen years of her life. As expected, the court set a hearing to hear the agreement we made. What wasn't expected was that the man asked for full physical custody.

Number Three hired a lawyer and was determined to take our son from me and divide my family. His fear of paying child support to me for the next eighteen years was the only reason he fought for full custody. I ended up losing my job as a school bus driver due to me taking too many days off for court and trying to find the past arson reports and any other thing I could use against him in court so that he could not be allowed to get custody of our son. I agreed to joint and gave him physical custody, only because my son really wanted to live with him. I knew that his dad loved him, and the Lord had also given me peace about it. My only real problem with the change was that I didn't want my boys separated or without that close knit bond siblings tended to have for one another.

But I really felt like the Lord showed me that he was just sending me help and gave me confirmation that allowing our son to live with his dad at the age of seven wasn't such a bad idea after all. Number Three was a decent dad to my son, but it wasn't long before he started saying mean things about me and trying to brainwash my son against me. Once he met back up with his high school crush, he began to get brutal with his words and started telling his family and anyone who'd listen that he was the only one providing for our son and that I did nothing but birth him. His sister and mother followed suit and have been giving me shade as well to this day. Someone actually convinced my son that his grandmother should be at his graduation instead of me, because he only had two tickets and they felt that she was been there for him more than I had been.

Boy, oh boy! The Lord had to show up and on time! I prayed and cried out to the Father like never before. I was livid! How dare I be excluded from my own child's High School Graduation? It was the defining moment in my life where the Lord heard my cry ,and within twenty-four hours of my prayer and the day of the event, my son called, saying he was on the way to deliver me my ticket. Shortly after that victory—in Christ Jesus!—Number Three's girlfriend would start with her annoying posts and comments on my son's Facebook page.

She was declaring that she was his mom now and listing all the tasks she had performed pertaining to our son. Every time she'd post what she did for my son, I would reply on his page, "Thank you," and remind her that I lived less than a mile away from their house. That if she had any issues with fulfilling the tasks Number Three had required of her, I was just a phone call away. Moreover, all her kids were grown and it seemed strange to me that she would want to take on another woman's responsibilities just to keep me at bay. She wanted Number Three and our son all to herself, and just like the others before her, my identity alone, caused uproar.

My son tried to run away from his dad's house one time and called me to come pick him up from school. The girlfriend had noticed how things were missing after he left in the morning and immediately notified his dad. They both met me at the school, and the moment I saw her, I informed the school officials that they were not married yet and I did not want her in the room with us while discussing our child. She looked at me and said the worst thing you can say to an overprotective mother. She stated that I didn't do anything for him, and she was more his mom than I was. Mind you, it was only her second or third year into the relationship with his father.

Before I knew it, I had brutally threatened her, and the school officials thought I was a threat and called the police. She waited outside

Unconditional 2, Four by Four – The Baby Daddy Drama Trauma

the room as requested, but his father ran out after her with total disregard to the purpose of the meeting. I was livid, because this was the second time this woman had somehow persuaded his dad to abandon my son due to my presence. The first time was when we were at a football game one day, and the coaches wanted all the parents to join their child on the field. Because I was there already, Number Three left with her right as they were getting ready to announce our names.

My son looked up to show them where his dad was, and they both were gone. I hugged my baby and told him, "No worries. Mama will always be here for you, no matter what," and we held hands and walked across the field together as the Lord saw fit. I will never forget that day. Even I couldn't believe that Number Three actually left to run after the insecure, codependent, insane woman. Right in the middle of his son being honored in the center field in front of everyone who had worked so hard throughout the whole football season. Now I understand how his now thirty-year-old daughter has become estranged and brokenhearted with pain ever since I left him years ago.

Just to sum up this baby daddy drama-trauma, Number Three had managed to talk, or should I say, buy me into an entanglement, tried taking full custody of our son, sent my ex a letter to destroy whatever dealings we may have had, and then continued to tell our son lies about me and forced him to choose between us on every occasion. When they say age ain't nothing but a number, here's one reason why I believe it. He was at least five older than me, initiated this proposition, and, in the end, couldn't handle it. I pray every day that God continues to protect me and my children from those who would even think of trying to come between a mother and her cubs. Also, praying for those who intentionally set out to assassinate someone else's relationship for their own benefit.

I realize that I was wrong as well for accepting such propositions, and the lengths we'd go in desperation. Let me explain my thinking and opinions of this dysfunctional arrangement and the lesson learned. I initially refused the indecent proposal, but out of a desperate need for safe housing and transportation, I considered the offer. It seemed easier to take money from men to survive and still be at home with my children than to leave them with strangers to go off to work for the entire day. Not including the childcare expenses that pretty much took up half of a minimum wage paycheck.

I always felt like if I told a man at least three times that I was not interested, the fourth time, he would have to pay me for my time and my frustration. I am sorry if this sounds a bit cold, but how many times have I had to find ways to repeat myself respectfully without getting slapped? Men tend to get even more aggressive when they see a strong woman with boundaries. Imagine every day of your life you are constantly being propositioned, delayed, detoured, and distracted from your agenda due to men being overly aggressive and not accepting no for an answer. Sadly, the work I put into turning guys away was so exhausting that it became the job and the paycheck for me.

Unconditional 2, Four by Four – The Baby Daddy Drama Trauma

The moment I said I was unavailable, their responses would be, "Eatin' ain't cheating", or "He doesn't have to know a thing". Or maybe even, "You need this money right here. I just want fifteen minutes of your time. Please?" The majority of the time I would refuse and stand strong; it was those low days, giving up days, when I would even entertain the thoughts. On the one hand, these men are of another species and I think it's the chase of it all but also desperation at its finest as well. Think about it, what kind of man would pay a woman his hard-earned money just to be acknowledged, loved, or even touched by a particular woman they know would not normally find them interesting?

What state of mind could you be in to offer someone your mouth on them while knowing nothing about them or their health condition? This kind of desperation can be very dangerous, not only for you but also for your children. When is it okay to pay for love and affection? What happens when you no longer want to engage? Will the payer or buyer walk away free and clear, or feel used and taken advantage of?

Can this arrangement get out of control, and how so?

Men can become very dangerous if they feel you used them or threw them away without care. Sometimes it can take up to a year or longer before they are able to see you with another man without starting a fight. The point is there's a lot more at stake than you initially think of when contemplating indecent proposals. Moreover, don't ever devalue yourself or sell yourself short, because you are priceless. There is no amount of money that could measure up to your worth. Nevertheless, I am forever thanking God that we are covered by the blood of Jesus. **Isaiah 54:17KJV:** "No weapon formed against me and my children shall prosper because ... nay, in all these things we are more than conquerors through him that loved us."

However, I must take a moment to reflect on my experiences with these other women and men after me. We call them "FenaBees" (meaning: you are on the <u>fence to be</u> the next or <u>going to be</u> <u>next in line</u>). I feel that someone needs to set the tone, and make it plain and clear of your role when entering a broken family. First and foremost, when a man or woman with children is interested in dating you, that does not mean the children are in need of another mother or father, for the most part. Please do not insert yourselves into the children's lives without an invite from one of the biological parents. Always seek to get both parents' approval when applicable, to prevent overstepping parental boundaries.

Know what those boundaries are before entering a relationship with someone with children. Ladies and gents, once again, we did not leave a great situation, and if you got my leftovers, I gave them to you on a silver platter. Please don't ever think that I would share my man with another woman, secretly, at no time. Stop thinking the baby mama wants him back or is sneaking around with him! Personally, I truly believe, no disrespect, that if I did want any of my baby daddies back, these women would not be living in the same house with them, period!

Unconditional 2, Four by Four – The Baby Daddy Drama Trauma

The funny part is, if these men had any valor at all, I would have never left them in the first place. What woman doesn't want a two-parent home for her children? Think about it, ladies. Most women would say that it just didn't work out for you. Really? Do you really believe we left our children's father because of the chemistry or connection? The chemistry was perfect; that's why a child was produced.

One last time, for all the "fentabees," most of us left these men for one reason only. They did not love or put the children ahead of their own desires. If a man can't love his own seed, then how can he love you, me, or anyone for that matter? Again, I didn't leave any good men. I left a few womanizers, narcissists, domestic abusers, child neglecting, and low-life, non-faith walking male species in the hell they were trying to put me and my children in, period. I understand someone's trash is another's treasure, but when there are children involved, the trash just stinks really, really bad.

As for the men entering into a broken family, if we wanted any one of our baby daddies, you would not be an issue. These kids and their mothers/fathers were here long before you and it is a package deal. If you can't trust that I want to be with you and only you, then find someone without children. How dare any one of you decide that the children's mothers or fathers are not allowed over to the house? Please stop with the insecurities, and find someone that you don't have to share with multiple people, please.

Also, be aware of those parents that try to publicly list all the things they have sacrificed or provided for their own child. It's impossible, and those who attempt to do so, especially on social media, have other children that they do nothing for, seem to be the fake, intimidated, and the insecure parent with a lot to hide.

I will say that, in spite of all the irritants and challenges along the way, I am still grateful and thankful for Number Three's commitment to look after and for providing for our son in all the ways that he was supposed to.

Thankfully, our son has recently graduated high school and left for college, so the drama ends here for now. I give all glory and honor to God for giving me peace. There's no longer a need to engage with Number Three or his wife in any way whatsoever. My faith has brought me to a point that I hold no ill will toward the fathers, their wives, or anyone for that matter. Today, I am able to forgive, and look forward to what's to come in the near future.

I pray that I am forgiven as well, and that **Proverbs 2:6 KJV:** "For the Lord gives wisdom; from his mouth comes knowledge and understanding," is true. That, one day, we as co-parents stand strong no matter what the challenge is and be supportive of one another's authority in their child's life.

However, I feel that parents should always keep in mind that once a child matures to the level of understanding the drama, they will revisit this foolishness and get clarity on the type of person you really are, and let's hope it's positive. Lessons learned here are that I will respect my body, demand respect from others, and continue to be a positive, uplifting, and loving force in my children's lives and the lives of others.

TRAUMA

Chapter Four
THE DRAMA TRAUMA

I met Number Four on a desperate mission to sow my royal oats after living in abstinence for almost six years. It was the longest time I had ever abstained from sex, and I was afraid that I was losing all my femininity. My walk seemed to get heavier and I just did not feel sexy anymore. There was a heating and cooling program opening up at the local University, and I thought I was sure to find my victim there. I say victim because I had only one thing in mind, and that was to fulfill every imagination I had put into subjection over the last six years.

I was in full lust mode and ashamed to say that I actually planned the entire entanglement with this man even though I knew he was in a relationship. My body convinced me that I only needed to borrow this guy for a short time, considering we both were a part of the ministry at our separate churches and needed to be discreet about it all. The plan was to knock my edge off the weekend his girlfriend was going out of town. I explained to him that I hadn't had sex in six years, and exactly what I needed to happen and for how long. Being very explicit, letting him know all the ways I wanted it, and in ways he had never even experienced before.

I had this guy doing all kinds of things that only a pornographic diabolical freak would even dream of. It was about six years' worth of pent up unadulterated, dominatrix, pull my hair and call me a b**h type of thoughts racing all around inside of me.

It all began the moment I was able to get him sized up, to be sure it would be worth my time. We were on a class break for lunch and he was about to walk into the men's restroom. Then I asked, "Do you need any help with that?"

He turned, looked at me, smiled, and said, "Certainly."

I immediately slipped into the men's restroom, walked into the stall with him, and locked the door. As he prepared himself, I held it while he peed, shook it off, and then looked up at him with a smile.

The next thing I knew, I started going to his house to do homework in hopes of seducing this man. It had been so long since I had been attracted to anyone, and my body wanted him for just one night ... or three. I was determined to give my body what it needed, but I will never forget what he told me right before I took my clothes off.

He said that he didn't deserve me, that I was a good girl, and he did not want to hurt me. It was yet another warning sign, and I wish now that I had listened and took heed. It was sure to be the worst and scariest entanglement I had ever found myself in. The kind of baby daddy drama trauma I experienced in this entanglement would be the defining moment that caused me to reevaluate everything in my life and make some serious changes. I learned that when someone shows you who they really are, believe them.

Number Four worked at his church as well, and one day, he found a necklace while cleaning the building. He brought it me, asked if I wanted it. It was cute, so I told him yes. When I turned around to allow him to put it on, I remember feeling a sharp object in the center of my back and he said to me, "If you ever take this off, I will have to kill you," and laughed. I turned around to see what he had in his hand, and it was one of those small steak knives with the brown handle. I should've known then that I was in a dangerous situation, but I wanted a taste of this bad boy anyway.

Although we agreed to only see each other a few times, his girlfriend ended up catching him at my house immediately after our first rendezvous and all hell broke loose from that point on. Number Four dropped me off at home that day after school because my car was on a flat and I didn't have time to fix it before class. As he was stepping off my porch to leave, his girlfriend pulled up and parked right next door, going to my neighbor's house. It was the funniest thing because I was talking out my top window at him when they ran into each other in the parking lot.

She looked at him and said, "Hey bae. What you doing over here? Give me a kiss."

I instantly ducked down inside the window, because I didn't want to see him kiss her right after we just had sex. But to my surprise, I heard her shouting, "What? Oh, so this is your new b**h's house?"

He said, "Yeah, this is my new woman, and do not call her a b**h! She is a good, respectable woman!"

She got even madder, and he told her to leave or he would remove her. Then he looked up at me in the window and said he'd call me later.

I was in shock, and I never expected him to break up with her right there and tell her about me. Because of the brutal and cold way he ended their relationship in front of me, I began to wonder how dangerous was this guy? They eventually made up after that, and only a few weeks later, I became pregnant. The moment I told him I was pregnant, him and his girlfriend immediately filed a PPO (personal protection order) to prevent me from coming to his job and or his home. The judge requested a hearing due to the obvious frivolous claims, and I can remember feeling so embarrassed to be over forty and still being told to have an abortion and it isn't my baby.

My friend Crystal went to court with me, and I just wanted to tell the judge that the order was an attempt to save his relationship with his girlfriend and it was not needed at all. He showed up with his girlfriend, and I looked at him in disbelief. I told the judge that I was not aware that I was not wanted near him or his job and had no problem staying away. I also reassured the judge that the baby was his and that paternity and child support would be sought after in the coming months ahead. The order was granted, and I stayed away up until my seventh month of pregnancy.

Once I learned that the baby would be a beautiful baby girl, I was so excited and just needed to know if it was at all possible for my baby girl to have a father. Yes, after three boys and three baby daddies, this was the first time I ever wanted to work something out with one of my child's fathers. I was about seven months and decided to do a drive by his job, hoping to see him outside so that I could tell him that I was having a girl. There he was outside as expected, cutting grass outside the church. I pulled up, rolled the window down, and proceeded to beg him not to call the police and tell them that I was there, violating the order.

He jokingly said, "Yep, I'm calling right now."

I explained to him that I just found out that the baby was a girl and I was so excited that I just had to ask him one more time if there was anything we could do to ensure my daughter could have a daddy, in spite of the circumstances. After showing him all the ultrasound pictures, we went inside and he continued to clean the building. Once he began cleaning the bathrooms, he went inside the stall and sat on the toilet, top down, and called me to come to him.

I walked over to him, and he said, "I never had sex with a pregnant woman before. Can I see what it feels like?"

I looked at him in confusion. I was so glad to be able to talk with him, and quickly pulled my panties down, lifted up my dress, and sat down on him in the stall. We both just started laughing at the sight of us on the toilet, humping in the church school bathroom. Lord father God, please forgive us for the disregard of our surroundings, and wash us both clean from our sins! In Jesus Name.

He and his girlfriend had been together for almost two years, they were unable to get pregnant, and she was understandably jealous, but also livid about mine.

His girlfriend was known in the neighborhood as a force to be reckoned with, and before I knew it, she began the taunting and placing broken glass on my doorstep as a warning to not have the baby. Lots of threatening calls, telling me that my baby would not make it to see day light. My neighbors happened to be her best friend's nieces and they also joined her in terrorizing me every day, all the way up to my delivery. One day, when I was crossing the street in front of my apartment, a car came out of nowhere and tried to run me over. I never saw it coming and I tried to run, but I was so big in my pregnancy, that I could barely walk.

Everyone saw her and her truck coming for me, and at that point, I decided to get a (PPO) Personal Protection Order on her! Things calmed down a bit until the day I went into delivery. I had just returned home from church and decided to order a pizza with everything on it. I ate two slices and then felt a pop while lying in bed.

Unconditional 2, Four by Four – The Baby Daddy Drama Trauma

Then fluid started to gush out, so I immediately jumped up and headed to the shower.

I called Number Four, and he stated he was on his way to take me to the hospital. From the moment we arrived at the hospital, his girlfriend called over and over. There was a man leaving out the emergency door in a wheelchair, and before the man could get out of the chair all the way, Number Four quickly snatched the chair from the man and gave it to me. I thought maybe he was nervous, but I did hear his phone ringing like crazy the whole time. After they got me situated into a room, he told me that he had to leave and would be right back.

I never thought I would be having my baby all by myself, but Number Four didn't come back until the next morning, with two duffle bags. The girlfriend had thrown his things out from her house and he ended up sleeping at the hospital in my room until it was time to go home with the baby. I believe the moment he saw her, he fell in love, because she looked just like him. He immediately stepped up, called, and stoped by to check on the baby every day, and his girlfriend eventually started to calm and be more accepting as well.

Except, they somehow thought I would give them custody of our daughter and let them raise her. I was so appalled at the absurd idea, that I didn't even give it a second thought or response.

One day, Number Four and I were at my townhouse, upstairs in my room, changing the baby diaper and having a brief conversation about the circumstances. He said something to me again about his girlfriend keeping our baby and, all of a sudden, those reflexes of mine got the best of me once again. As he was trying to finish his sentence, my hand just reached up and slapped him in the mouth so quick, I never saw it coming. Immediately, we began to tussle as I grabbed for his hands, to keep him from hitting me back. It wasn't long before my three sons were beating down the door and trying to get in the room.

Luckily, I was able to calm everybody down and explain that it was my fault, and apologized for slapping Number Four before things got out of control.

After about a month or so, I woke up one morning to Number Four standing over the baby with a Q-tip in her mouth. I knew what he was doing, but wondered why he was sneaking a DNA test. I would have gladly taken one for him with no questions asked. So, I then asked to see his DNA kit and assisted him in the swabbing of her mouth and mine, too, ensure that the specimen was gathered properly.

Although I hadn't had sex with anyone other than him in the last six years, I wasn't offended at all because I needed him and everyone else to be sure about how to treat my child.

That has always been my attitude on the issue of paternity. I'm the one always making sure the father has no excuse to not take care of his own seed and allowing opportunities to share in responsibilities of the children.

Before the results were back, Number Four had rented a house not far away and wanted us to move in it. I thought it was very sweet of him, and the results of the DNA test arrived the same day we were loading my furniture into the U-Haul truck.

He walked over to me and said, "Look what I got! And if this isn't my baby, you are not moving in this house today."

The results read ninety-nine point nine, of course, and we continued to load the truck and finished moving that day, which was my Valentine's Day Gift.

The things that happened in that house have replayed in my head over and over through the years, and I just feel the need to share with you and anyone else that will listen. Life is too short and we must take the time to do the research and background checks on these men before we have their babies and move our children in with them. Dating an abusive man can not only cost you your life but also the custody of all your children for staying with him too long.

Can I repeat that, ladies? You can lose physical custody of all your children for just simply staying with an abusive man too long.

It wasn't until after me, my boys, and our new baby girl had moved into this new house that I was told my fate. I was called into the bedroom one day; Number Four then opened the top drawer and pulled put our rental lease agreement. He turned to me and said, "You see this?" and ripped it into pieces. Then he stated, "Everything I previously agreed to was a lie and there is going to be changes around here, and if you don't like it, you and your kids can leave. But you can't take my baby with you."

He also mentioned that he did a lot to win me over and now that he had me, it was finally time for him to get back to being himself and the lifestyle he really lived. I was told that he was in love with his girlfriend, he was going to move back in with her around the corner, he would pay half of all the bills, and I should be happy that I had a man willing to help out and move me out of the projects. I could've peed my pants, then. I immediately called my apartment management and told them that I was not able to move out on the specified date originally stated in the thirty day vacate notice. I was livid for him to even think I was willing to be his kept whore nanny while he slept with another woman around the corner from our home. Moreover, he thought he would have keys to my house and come and go as he pleased.

The girlfriend even worked two streets over at a nearby beauty shop and she would ride past all day every day, commuting back and forth to work. It was one incident after the other with this man.

One time during an argument, Number Four went outside in the backyard and picked up a two by four. He walked toward and me and said, "Get your weapon." I was in total disbelief and started to laugh. He said, "Alright, if you don't get your weapon, you are about to get knocked out with this one."

I started to look around to find something and then I saw another two by four and picked it up.

"Come on, b**h!" he yelled.

Unconditional 2, Four by Four – The Baby Daddy Drama Trauma

I looked at him and saw that he was not kidding and really wanted to hurt me. I just dropped the stick and ran, having no clue why he wanted to fight me like that. We continued to argue every day in that house, and most of the time, I'd never really knew what for.

The first time I tried to leave with our daughter, he grabbed her by the feet of her snowsuit and tried pulling her from my hands. I remember thinking, *I will never give up my baby girl,* and I was willing to fight him to the end. He snatched so much of my hair out that day, I eventually lost all my beautiful long hair I had grown during pregnancy.

That was the first time he went to jail for abusing me. The police told him that he could not return home, and he was livid because it was his house, too.

After his girlfriend paid his bail, he showed up at the house on a bicycle and wanted to apologize. It was funny, because we had a long discussion about the incident, he apologized, we had sex, and made up. Then, about an hour later, the police knocked on the door and told him to come outside. They arrested him again for returning to the house but eventually had the case thrown out and we were back at it again.

I remember on my birthday—I forget which one—the landlord that lived next door asked me if I wanted to go out with her to this local bar. I told her yes because Number Four and I had been arguing the whole day about what I wanted to do with my seventy-five-dollar jury duty check I was waiting for in the mail. He got so mad that I wanted to get my hair done and just wanted me to be miserable at home, broke, because we had a lot of bills and other things needed for the home. While I was getting dressed to leave out with the landlord, Number Four had started taking everything I owned out of our bedroom and started throwing them in another room all over the place.

Then after he removed all of my things from the bedroom, he began taking things out of the refrigerator that I bought and throwing the food everywhere all over the clothes, shoes, hair and health care products, on the bed and the floor, everywhere. By the time he finished throwing everything that belonged to me in the house into that one room, it was a big, nasty pile almost as high as the ceiling. From the pots and pan to the curtains and just any and everything that belonged to me. Almost every day he'd do something evil and mean, like turning off the water so that no one could use the bathroom or shower, just to get us to leave the house.

One time, I was coming home from the grocery store, and he got mad at me and told me I could not put the groceries in his refrigerator, and I might as well take all the groceries back to the store. It was hard to save for another place to live right after I had just given the landlord two months' rent in advance. Besides that, I had allowed one of my friends to stay at the apartment with her children. She was so mad at me for having to come back home, but I had no other choice. He was too abusive.

The drama I experienced with that man had caused me to really do some soul searching to find out how I got myself into that situation and how I was going to get myself out of it. There was yet another time I had called, and he told me he was at the house with his co-worker doing something, but she was about to leave. I told him I was on my way, because I just wanted to be sure that there was no monkey business going on between them. When I walked in the door, the energy was too quiet, so I decided to play a little game just to see if she really wanted him and was trying to play it off. So, I went into the kitchen to get a glass of Kool-Aid, and on my way back to the living room, I walked up to her and whispered in her ear.

I said, "Girl, when you leaving? I'm trying to finish f**g my man really quick."

She almost turned red and immediately asked him if it were true. His eyes constricted, and he ground his teeth.

So, then I asked him, "Why are you mad at me? Are you screwing both of us?"

You know that fool said, "Yes, I am f*g both of y'all. What you going to do about it?"

I was holding my cup and my reflexes kicked in, sending my cup sailing through the air. It hit his chest, and the red Kool-Aid spilled everywhere.

He jumped up, and I just started running! The girl was even scared for me and she started chasing him to stop him from hurting me. I would like to thank her for that. She saved me that day, yet I still went outside and called him and her some names I can't even spell. I left them both there for a few minutes until I realized that she was still trying to linger. I drove back over there, demanding all our daughter's clothes and furniture, just to have him busy for a while. She finally left once she saw that I was not going anywhere for a minute.

Again, with the drama.

It was another late night, and I had decided to show Number Four his phone and that I could see that he had been talking to his ex all day. As I was trying to wake him up, my reflexes got the best of me again and I accidently dropped the phone on his face and he woke up ready to kill. I tried asking him about the number in his phone, but he thought I just smacked him in the face with the phone and began chasing me around the house again. I think that night was when he put me out the house, two in the morning, with no shoes, purse, or car keys while my kids were in the bed sleeping. It was the most embarrassing moment, because I actually stood outside at the corner of our street and waited for the police for about three to four hours, no shoes on, scared, and it was dark. I was calling everyone, hoping anyone would pick up at that time of hour.

When the police finally arrived, they actually told me to leave and grab the kids in the morning. I was so pissed because Number Four had written a note and taped it to the front door and slammed it in our faces and the cops did nothing. The note said something like, **Get off my front porch and take her with you**, and they seemed to be more afraid of him than I was.

Soon after, my friend pulled up to get me, and I can remember being so embarrassed because I didn't even have shoes on and had to leave everything. I left with my friend to avoid waking my children up to the trauma.

The next morning, Number Four was all giggles as if nothing ever happened.

Eventually, I moved out and got another house very close by. I think we tried the friend thing for a while until I wanted to have other men over. I will never forget the day my new guy friend and Number Four bumped heads at my house. It was perfect! This guy was fine, and had diamonds dripping from his fingers and his neck. He was the black chocolate I love so much and definitely a keeper for sure.

It was his first time over to visit, and he pulled up in a brand-new blue and chrome Ford-350, and he had on a royal blue, crushed velvet adidas jogging suit with a white Kango, and white top ten snickers on his feet, baby.

He was truly a chocolate fantasy come true, and it was something to see when Number Four pulled up and saw him walking into my house.

Number Four started stuttering, stalling, and making up stuff to hang around a little longer. Later, when he returned our daughter, he asked to speak with me privately, and I heard the words that every woman would love to hear after showing your ex the new guy. He declared and decreed that he loved us, wanted us back, and was willing to fight for his family!

He told me that he would marry me, and wanted to buy a house together and start over. We then put our money together, bought a house, and started to build a life together. Unfortunately, it just wasn't in the cards for us and, believe me, I tried everything to make that relationship work out for the sake of our daughter. I endured lots of little petty things. He would stop the washer and only pull out my clothes, then place them on the back porch. Lock me out of the house in my underwear. All kinds of annoying things.

One time, I was sleeping in the bed with my daughter and Number Four just snatched me by my ankles and started dragging me toward the door.

"You're getting out my house, right now! Always making a mess."

All I knew was I was terrified to be waked up like that, and as I began to tussle with him to get loose, he somehow slipped in the kitchen and broke his toe. It was a right on time karma, and it was really funny because he already had a cast on each arm from a previous slip and fall accident.

Unfortunately, that didn't stop the terrorizing drama. He even tried to make me jealous of the love, time, and attention he would give our daughter. He'd kiss her, tell her how special she was, while staring at me, in hopes to sense jealousy or some kind of reaction.

Unconditional 2, Four by Four – The Baby Daddy Drama Trauma

It was such a delight to see my daughter so happy with her dad. It was all I ever wanted for her, and all I really needed from him. I have always been a daddy's girl; I loved my dad, and I wanted my daughter to experience what we shared together. And as they did things together, I kindly stayed home and allowed my daughter to soak it all up. Because I knew darn well if I wasn't getting the attention, my daughter better have been getting it. He was always so angry with me, and I never knew why most of the time.

I would try to spoil him rotten to make sure he didn't get upset, just to keep him from fighting in front of the children all the time. Making sure he was satisfied in and out of the bedroom ... and still he found a way a start a fight with me. Nothing was good enough and he stayed grumpy all the time. It was very depressing being with him most of the time, because he always seemed to be too tired, angry, and frustrated every day.

He would sometimes even include our daughter in his anger with me by saying things like, "Your mother is a B***h. You don't need a mother, and I'm going to find you a better mother."

Or his favorite, "When I get my lawsuit money, we are going on a vacation together and Mommy can't come with us."

I knew deep down in my heart that God did not send me this man and He would not allow a man to abuse me like that. After various police reports made against him and several court hearings, I was told by a judge that if she saw either one of us back in her courtroom with any more foolishness, she would take our daughter from the both of us. That was when I knew for sure that there could be no more incidents. I was not willing to lose custody of my children for a man that obviously did not want me. My plan to escape was like no other and I still laugh to this day about how it all went down.

I know that he was pissed, because of how he responded the first time I did my first disappearing act on him. The first time, it was the first few weeks I had known him and we were at his house when I felt the need to just disappear. It was early morning; we had just finished having sex and he received a phone call. During the call, he left the room and lowered his voice, and I knew it was his ex. I thought I had heard him saying that he was on his way and immediately I freaked out and left, walking home from his house.

It was funny because I was new to the neighborhood and got lost on the way home and it took me about an hour when I was only a few blocks away. He told me later that he went driving around looking for me and was puzzled as to where and why I had left so abruptly and made me promise to never do it again.

Well, my second from the last and final goodbye was just as abrupt. But, hey, at least I gave him a goodbye gift that time. But before I tell you about that, let me share one last trauma that ultimately forced me to leave in fear for my life and enter a domestic violence homeless shelter that helped me get my life back on the right track, and thank you, God, for your direction!

Unconditional 2, Four by Four – The Baby Daddy Drama Trauma

One morning, as I was getting our daughter ready for school and to walk her to the corner school bus stop, Number Four told me we needed to talk. As he said that to me, he was grabbing his gun from the dresser and slowly placing it in his pants. He said that he needed to see that I had been looking for work, and that I must quit my college courses to help him pay the bills. He went on to say that I better be able to show him that I had been looking for work or we were going to have it out as soon as I put the baby on the bus. Then, he got in his truck and left, saying he'd be right back.

Immediately, after my neighbor and I put our children on the bus, I began to walk with her to her porch, asking her if she thought I should be afraid when he came back. I had told her what he had said to me before he left, and expressed to her that I was confused and needed help. I couldn't decide if I should leave or stay. He thought that I was smoking weed every day and not looking for work, and he was pissed. I was smoking every day, but I was also looking for work.

Little did he know that I was looking to work, but only to leave his tail, because, obviously, he couldn't afford me. I didn't mind helping out but I felt like my money should have been extra. I was supposed to be a help mate after establishing something for me to help with, I thought. Nevertheless, I figured if I paid the rent then I would be the head of the household and everyone must listen to me and my rules. Furthermore, if I had more children than I could afford already, it would be wiser for me to prioritize in the children's best interest first.

I was livid to have been given an ultimatum to work or else. Never had I had a man express to me that he needed me to work in order to be with him. I was appalled and not interested at all in helping a man take care of me. It also seemed as though he was treating me like the type of child that did not want to do anything but sleep and eat. It was not my true intention at all.

As we sat on the neighbor's porch talking, Number Four pulled up.

We both watched him go into our house and come back out, looking for me. Once he saw me sitting on the porch, he then got in his truck and pulled up in front of my neighbor's house and said, "Get your mothaf**ing a** over here now!"

I looked at my neighbor and then looked back at him, and he began searching for something under his seat.

He said, "You better hurry up and give me my keys."

What keys?

But I was afraid that he was reaching for his gun to shoot at me on my neighbor's porch, so I just gave him my keys and ran back to her porch and sat down. He then pulled away, and I sat there asking my neighbor if she thought he was going to shoot up the whole house if I didn't give him my keys. She just looked at me, and I told her that I got to leave this man right now. I just couldn't allow him to take my keys and leave me locked out of the house again in my pajamas. I was too humiliated and embarrassed to keep going through this petty stuff every time he got mad with me.

The moment he pulled up, I called my close friend, Nee Nee, to come for me, and then my daughter's school to tell them that I would be there shortly to pick her up. I also told them that it would be her last day and we were leaving the state for our safety. I further explained that I was in a domestic violence situation and had to leave abruptly. Then, I went to the police station to obtain an escort to go with me back to the house to retrieve all of my belongings. We all pulled up at the house at the same time.

The police made him stand outside while I gathered as much as I could and put it into the trunk of my friend's car. Mind you, we had bought that house together and I had invested everything I had into the renovation and rehabilitation. It was a very hard lesson to learn about not putting your name on the deed of the house at the time of purchase. I left everything and took only a few bags of clothes that were too small and the clothes on our backs.

As I said earlier, my second from the last final goodbye was just as abrupt. But at least I gave him a goodbye gift this time, and it was one of my favorite grand exits.

By this time, I had learned how to pack up all of my important essentials and hide them so that he would not notice when I was leaving. I had been planning my escape for quite some time, but I never had the means to move the plan along without too many complications.

But time was seeming to never present itself in a suitable or convenient manner. Literally forced to step out on faith, with no real plan at all, totally depending on the goodness of the Lord. I called a dear old friend and told him what time, and where to meet me.

My friend was very worried about me being in such an abusive relationship, and he wanted to help me get away from it with my life fully intact. He bought me a one-way ticket to South Carolina so that my daughter and I would be safe for a while. Then handed me some money and told me to be ready! I waited till about twenty minutes before it was time to meet my friend at the corner, one street over from the house. There was at least six inches of snow outside, and I had too many bags to carry.

The snow was so high that it was hard to walk without slipping and stumbling. I gave Number Four a fifty-dollar bill and told him I wanted to BBQ some steaks, and to go get us some wine and things to go with it. He was so in shock that I had some money, that he just jumped up and went racing out the door. At the time, both of our cars were broken down and he had to walk one block over and two blocks down to the market. Once he hit the first corner, I grabbed my bags and my daughter and tried running as fast as I could.

I remember not getting anywhere because I kept dropping the bags and getting my feet stuck in the piles of snow. It felt like I was in a horror film, trying to run and kept falling, looking back and crying, thinking I was going to get caught. The fear I had in that moment

Unconditional 2, Four by Four – The Baby Daddy Drama Trauma

reassured me that I was indeed in a traumatic situation and needed out desperately. Once I made it to the corner to meet my friend, he was not there. I fell down in the snow and cried out. Damn, damn, damn!

I was crying so hard, and as I looked further down the street in the distance, I could see my friend's car stuck in the snow at the other corner. We then hid behind a dumpster in the alley and laid in the snow so that Number Four would not see us if he arrived back before I was gone. As I laid there in the snow, telling my daughter to please hold on a minute, I pulled out my phone and called my friend. He miraculously became unstuck from the ice hole and drove down to the alley where we were hiding. He got out the truck and opened the back doors to start putting the bags inside.

As I got ready to get up and get into his car, Number Four started walking up to the house and looked our way. I was so scared; I was shaking like booty meat! Once he turned his head to put the key inside the door, we hurried and jumped in the back seat of the car and ducked as low as we could. We saw him go inside and come back out, looking back and forward, as we left for the bus terminal. I was so scared and paranoid all the way to South Carolina. I felt like Number Four would jump out the bushes on me at any moment's notice.

My stay in South Carolina was short lived due to my lack of sharing abilities, and I went back to Michigan only after three months. On the second day of arriving back to the house with Number Four, he attacked me again out of fear. We were having a very minor disagreement with allowing our daughter to attend a pool party with some neighbors that he had just met a few months after we moved on the block. I walked to the door to look outside, and he ran for me and grabbed me by my hair and told me to go. He thought I was going to leave again, panicked, and snatched me bald just that quick.

I was so pissed that I had just got there and he was already putting his hands on me. After enrolling our daughter back into school and getting everything back in place, he decided that I was taking too long to find a job. That was when he stated he wanted to have that talk with me after our daughter was put on the bus that day. I will never forget how he would tell me all the time that I was not special and to quit expecting people to treat me like that. He told my daughter several times that she did not need a mother and that they should just leave mommy and never come back.

It was so hard to see myself getting out of that house and starting over again. It was even harder to leave the first home I ever purchased to go look for a homeless shelter to help me rebuild what I had so easily given up without a fight.

As we drove away, I started to remember what life was like when I had my own place, just me and kids. I felt the need to prove to myself that I could get it again and I was not and could not be stuck with this man, or any other man for that matter. When I arrived at my friend's house, I immediately started calling homeless shelters for help to get me back into my own place again.

Unconditional 2, Four by Four – The Baby Daddy Drama Trauma

I called day and night, looking for an empty bed, and after about two weeks, a domestic violence homeless shelter finally answered and offered my daughter and me a bed. I was told to meet them in a police parking lot at three o'clock in the morning and they would pick me up from there. Domestic violence shelters are very discreet locations for protection purposes, and I was not allowed to be dropped off by anyone. It seemed like forever trying to get signed into the shelter and given a room and key. My heart was so heavy. I could not wait to get to my room, put my daughter to sleep, and cry like a baby.

As I began to reflect on everything, my phone rang. It was a strange number, and I really didn't want to answer it because I only had a few hours to get my cry in before the princess woke again. Something said to answer it anyway, and it was the county law agency that I had previously done my college internship with a couple years back. They wanted to know if I would be interested in a Paralegal position at the firm. The pay would start at twenty-eight dollars and forty cents an hour.

The moment I faced the fear and stepped out on faith, the Lord had blessed me. He had given me a job and pay increase that I wasn't even qualified for at the time. The Lord really showed up and showed out for me. The whole time I lived at the shelter, I was able to save all of my checks, use emergency assistance to pay off all past utility bills, and begin to replace everything I had lost.

Tawana Roquall Fultz

Deuteronomy 30:3 NIV: "God, your God, will restore everything you lost; He'll have compassion on you; He'll come back and pick up the pieces from all the places where you were scattered."

Our entire stay at the Domestic Violence Homeless Shelter was completely mind blowing from the moment I attended my first domestic violence meeting. They had everyone sit in a circle of chairs and go around, one by one, introducing themselves. After your introduction, you were to tell how many abusers you had and also share a little bit about the day you decided to step out on faith and be brave enough to leave without a plan.

First off, I never thought I was in an abusive relationship.

I always thought that if a man did not hit me with his fist, then everything was okay. Mind you, this man was snatching me by my hair, closed a car door on my leg, spit in my face, and called my mom and everyone else in my family every name you can think of. Cursed me in front of my children, coerced several people to come terrorize me, and possibly even hurt me in front of our daughter. I can remember getting down on my knees in the middle of a fight and praying to the top of my lungs for God to stop him from wanting to fight all the time. He literally prayed with me, and told God that I was a B*** and that he'd better get me out of there soon.

As they went around the room, sharing their stories one by one, I could hear, see, and count all of my abusers as well. By the time it was my turn, I knew how many times I had been abused and when the abuse first started. Before I could open my mouth, tears began to roll down my face as I realized that I was a victim of domestic violence and for such a very long time. I could not get one single word out. My heart was so filled with sadness from not protecting myself.

How could I have allowed so many people to hurt me over and over again like that, without even stopping to cry?

The leader of the group meeting then explained to each and every one of us that we had suffered long enough and that our first thirty days there at the shelter would be focused on getting some rest. "Rest in your mind, your body, and your soul," she'd said.

They just wanted us to be free of all responsibilities and allowed us to do absolutely nothing but fun, rest, and relaxation. Then after that, I would begin to start rebuilding and preparing a space that I could thrive and flourish in with my children.

Philippians 4:8 KJV: "Finally, brethren, whatsoever things are true, whatsoever things are honest, whatsoever things are just, whatsoever things are pure, whatsoever things are lovely, whatsoever things are of good report; if there be any virtue, and if there be any praise, think on these things."

I would like to add that I am not, by any means, innocent in any of these traumatic circumstances, and I did not take all of this abuse sitting down. I aggravated and retaliated on many of these incidents, and I do know that two wrongs do not make a right. So, I will take a moment to apologize to all four of my baby daddies and say it was not meant to be, and it did not work out because of it. I have no regrets because of the wisdom, knowledge, and understanding I gained throughout the process. My God has taught me how to forgive and has begun the healing process in me.

There is not one angry, jealous, or bitter bone in my body for these men, and I continue to pray for them daily. I pray they will become the best men, fathers, and husbands they can possibly be, moving forward, and that they will continue to build their relationships with their children as they should. I also pray for the FenaBees, that they know their place and gradually enter in the broken homes with caution and care with only the children's best interest in mind. Moreover, I would like to share a few karmic events in my life that I think will further help the FenaBees moving forward. It is not meant to shame or belittle the next mate in line, but to bring awareness to some common mistakes of mixed interpretations.

While I won't mention names, in order to protect and respect those involved, I must share a few karmic lessons I've learned about entering into a broken family or relationship.

I once thought I could take a man from a woman. I simply decided that I wanted a man and didn't really care if he was available or not. It wasn't so much disregard to their significant others; it was more so me being a spoiled brat and thinking I could have anything I wanted no matter who it belonged to. Yeah, I've come a long way and I give all glory to God.

Unconditional 2, Four by Four – The Baby Daddy Drama Trauma

Any who, with this mindset, it can be the door opener to some major pain and experiences to enter your life. I found an interest in a guy and later found out that he was in a relationship. My first intentions were to respect that and move on. Unfortunately, my ego got in the way the moment I saw his girlfriend. For some strange reason, I always felt like if I looked better than the girlfriend then I was supposed to have him.

What a spoiled and self-centered brat I was. Yes, indeed. So, once I saw her and decided I was better looking, I would then feel I had the right to have him and not her. Now, after I had captivated her man, I would then tease her and laugh in her face when he was not looking, of course. I will never forget this particular time because the karma was so bad that it literally made me go back to her and apologize. I even begged her to take him back!

The man turned out to be the worst relationship I had ever experienced in my life. I was so traumatized that it took me at least three years to stop looking over my shoulder and checking my tires before I left the house. Like I said, I was broken down so bad that I went back to the ex-girlfriend and not only apologized but I cried in her arms, begging for her forgiveness. I knew I was being punished for hurting my fellow sister and disregarding her existence for no darn reason at all. My heart ached everyday until the moment we actually sat down and had this discussion.

We eventually became friends, and she even spends time with our daughter. She also came along with me on my jobs and helped out on several occasions. Thank you, Trice! I love you, woman, and I wish you all the happiness you are experiencing right now this very day. I also pray that the Lord Father God will bless you and your seeds to continue to grow and prosper in this life and in the next! In Jesus Mighty Name I Pray and Thank You! Amen.

Now on the flipside of this coin, I was also given this opportunity to be teased and disregarded concerning my relationship. Once that relationship began entering its ending stages, I moved out the house. After only about three weeks of me moving out, he had proposed to a young lady and she was all over the social media, smiling and grinning. Creating all kinds of subliminal posts about her come up. Attempted to bring harm to me, and even came to my home in the wee morning and keyed my truck.

All I could think about was the way I treated the girl before me, and I literally let her off the hook and never even pressed charges. The Lord has a way of revealing things to you and allowing you to vindicate a negative action made on your behalf. What I mean by that is, one week before the incident, I was given a scratch pin to start covering the scratches on my truck made by my son's friends and grocery store carts previously. It was revealed to me that I not only provoked the anger and conflict, but the Lord had already provided a repair pin weeks before she had come to key my car. It was up to me to understand that grace and extend it to her for the remission of my sins.

Furthermore, because I was receptive to correction, forgiveness, and redemption, the Lord also allowed me to see the reap of her karma as well.

It was only a few years later when the sister of the girlfriend contacted me on social media and poured out her heart and feelings of despair to get the guy away from her sister. She went on to confirm that (a) never tease the last girlfriend, (b) always hear out the ex, which it may be difficult due to manipulation, and (c) get all the information you can on him before you think you've found your Boaz! There is much to consider when you're FenaBee next!

Although hindsight is always clearer, as I reflect on many past relationships, I can see clearly how they affected me emotionally, mentally, physically, and spiritually. Lastly, May God forbid this from occurring, but when entering broken relationships, broken families, and/or broken homes, never forget the soul ties, curses, and strongholds that may also come along with it. Every relationship is not guaranteed to succeed, and every child born into those unsuccessful relationships isn't promised to be healthy. Let's do our research, ladies and gents, before we commit, and include our father God in everything.

Today, I love myself and I will not allow anyone else to ever hurt and abuse me ever again. While writing this book and the last, God has brought healing, restoration, and joy back into my life, and I am forever grateful that I can move on in peace not pain.

Finally, I pray that every child, woman, man whom may be affected by abuse of any kind may regain their strength in the Lord and get out and be safe as soon as possible. That they will feel the fear and do it anyway. In Jesus Name Amen.

Thanks for reading my story!

ABOUT THE AUTHOR

Photographer: Frankie Fultz

TAWANA ROQUALL FULTZ

Born in the City of Detroit, September 12, 1973, I love to help people and make folks smile. Making fun in traumatic situations to ease the pain is what I'm known for, and you probably have never seen me without my bubbly spark! Some say I'm loud, funny, but very serious when it comes to my spirituality, my children, and my respect.

Although I admit to many mistakes and poor choices in life, I am also admitting to not being perfect by any means. But I am willing to fight each and every day to live in my truth and strive to be a better human being.

I believe in the human family, and consider everyone a brother and sister outside of matrimony, and promise to continue to strive to be a better person and more pleasing to God, my father in heaven.

My idea of a perfect day is spending time with my now adultren, either making a family feast together or just singing karaoke around the living room.

Website Contact list:
Amazon.com: TAWANA ROQUALL FULTZ: Books, Biography, Blog, Audiobooks, Kindle
https://beableproducts4u.com
https://www.facebook.com/B-Able-Products-101780475156062
https://www.facebook.com/MsTawanaF
www.instagram.com/b_able_products4u
https://www.linkedin.com/in/tawana-fultz-6ab7b378/

https://www.goodreads.com/user/show/88015630-tawana-fultz

www.ingramcontent.com/pod-product-compliance
Lightning Source LLC
LaVergne TN
LVHW091317080426
835510LV00007B/522